ADULT COLORING BOOKS

DREAM CATCHER

VOLUME 2

STRESS RELIEVING PATTERNS

COLOR TEST PAGE

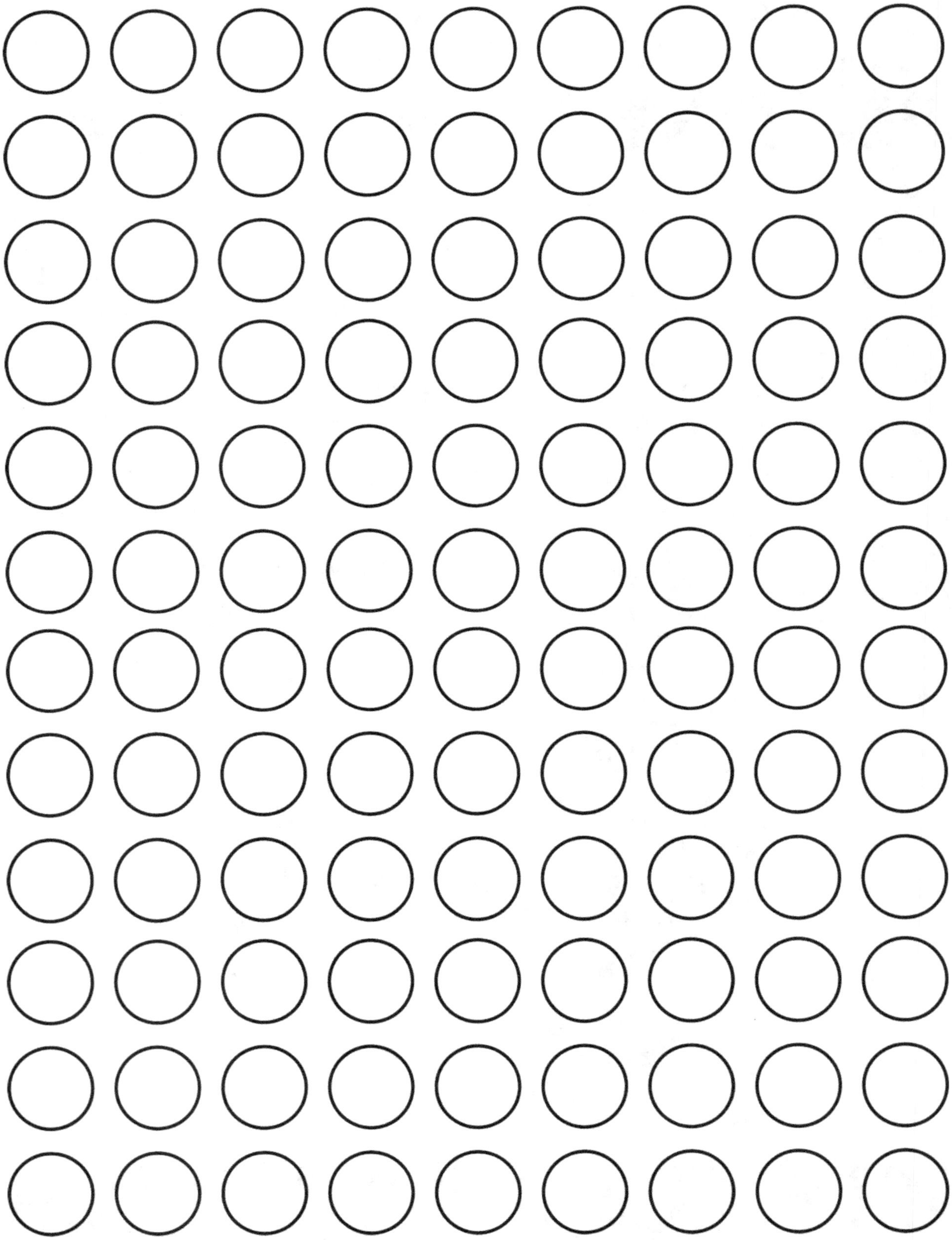

COLOR TEST PAGE

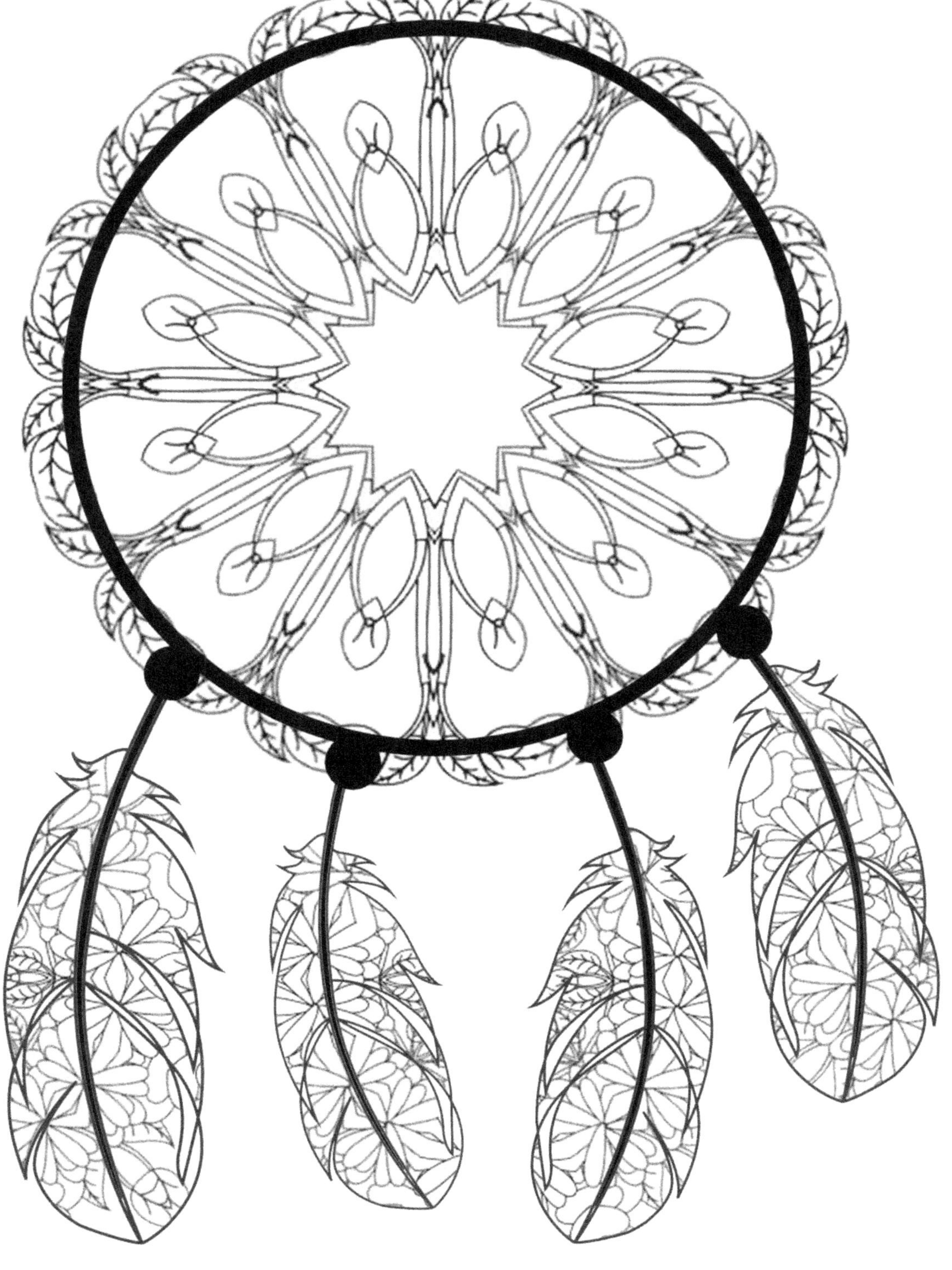

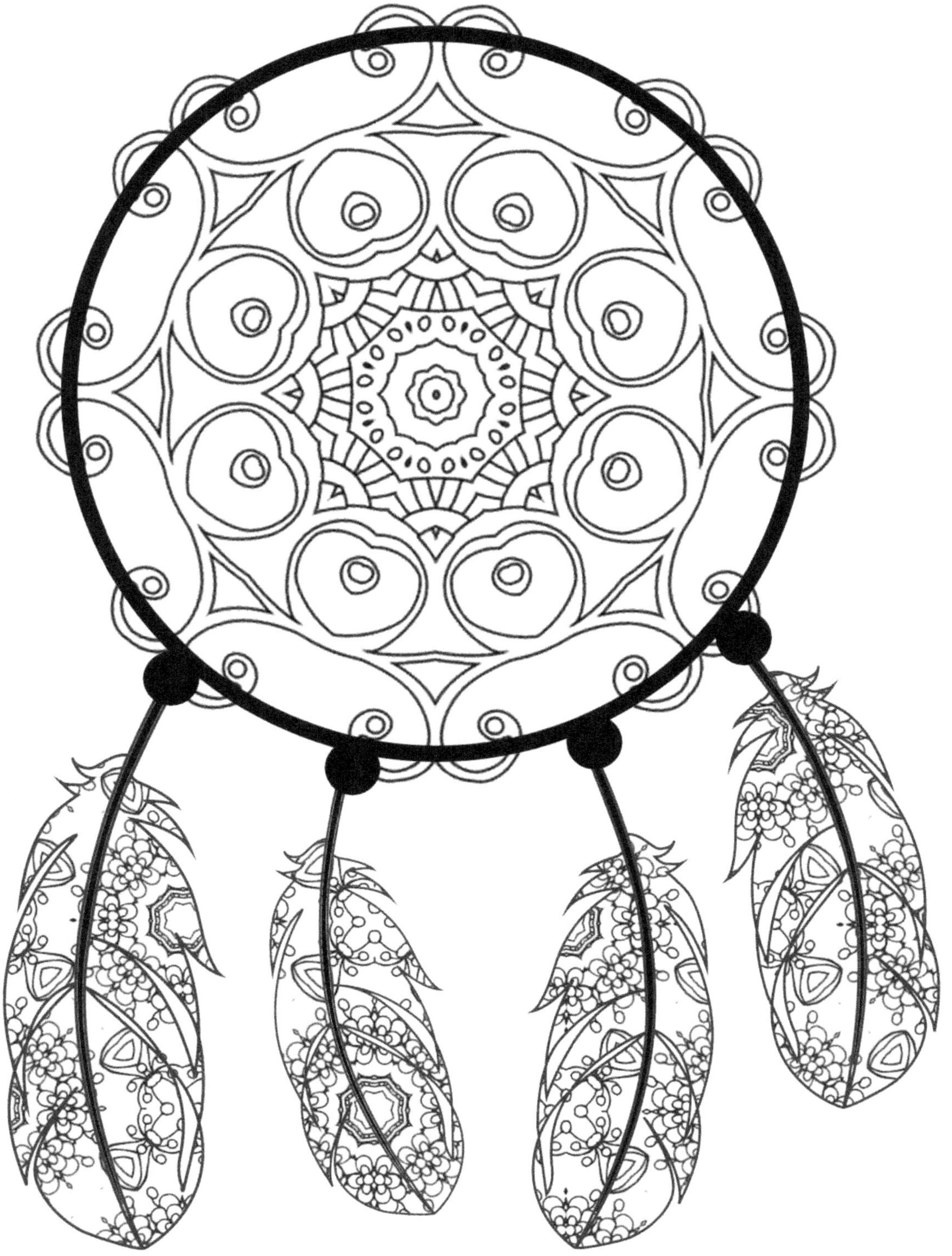

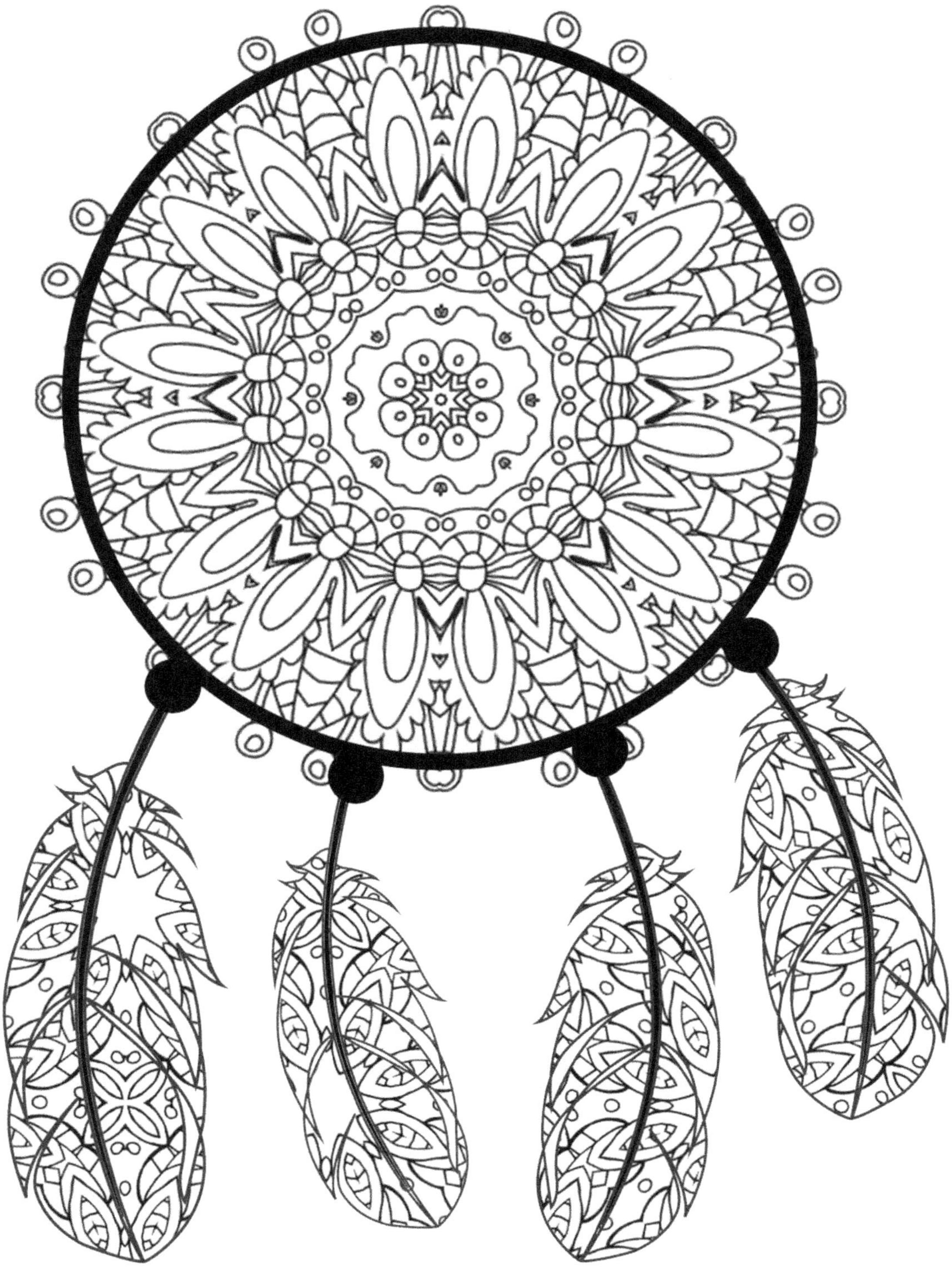

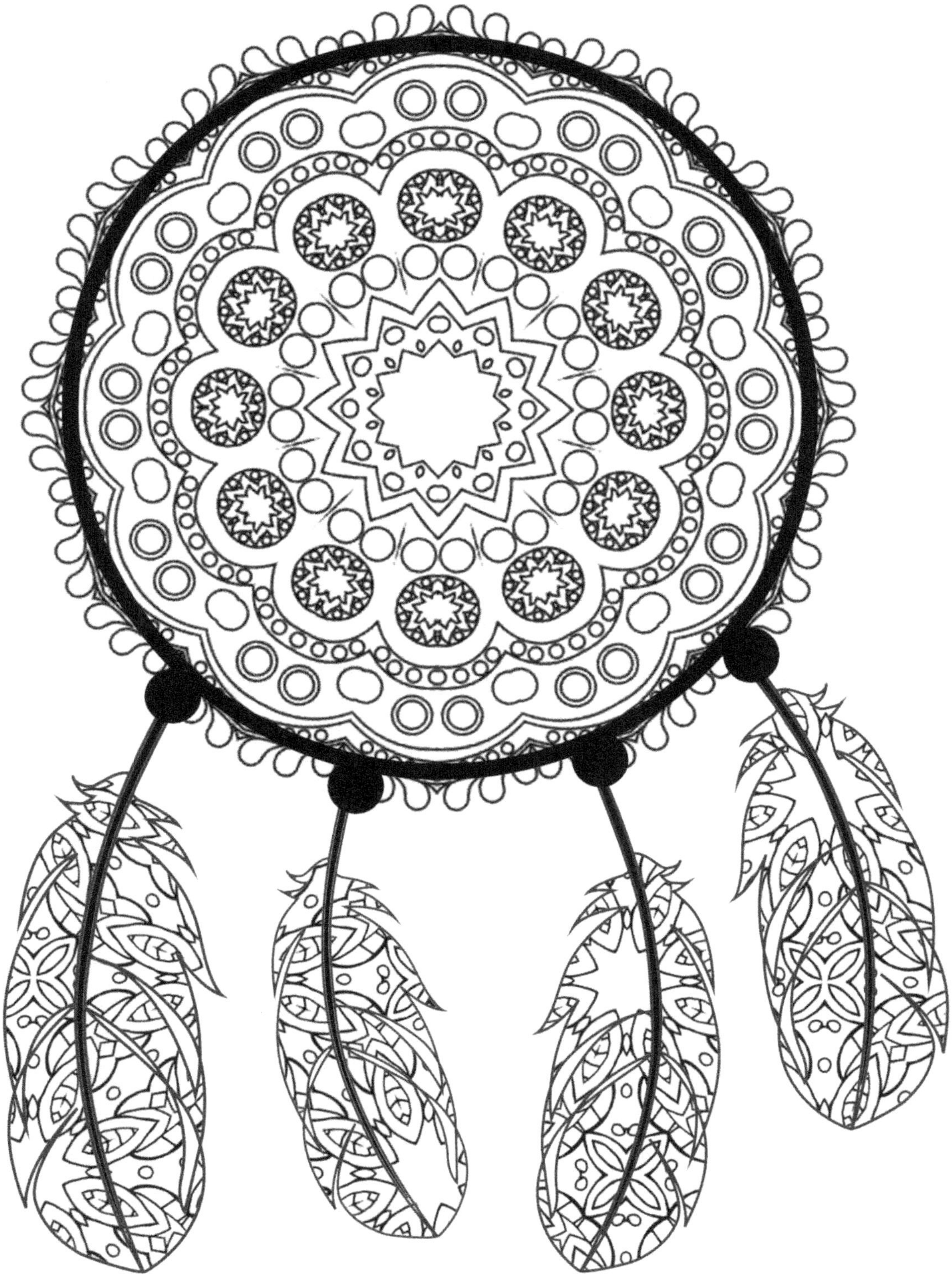

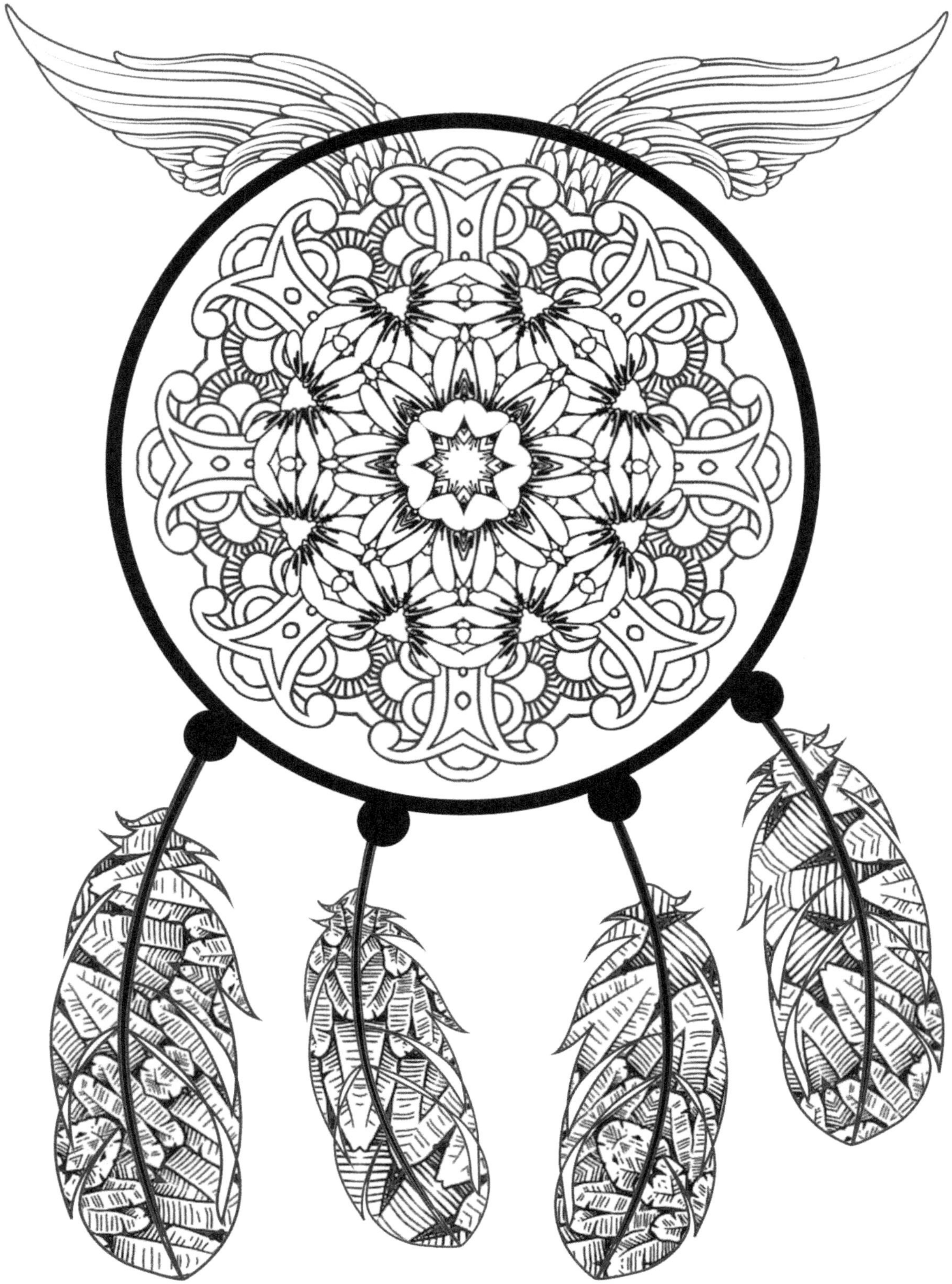

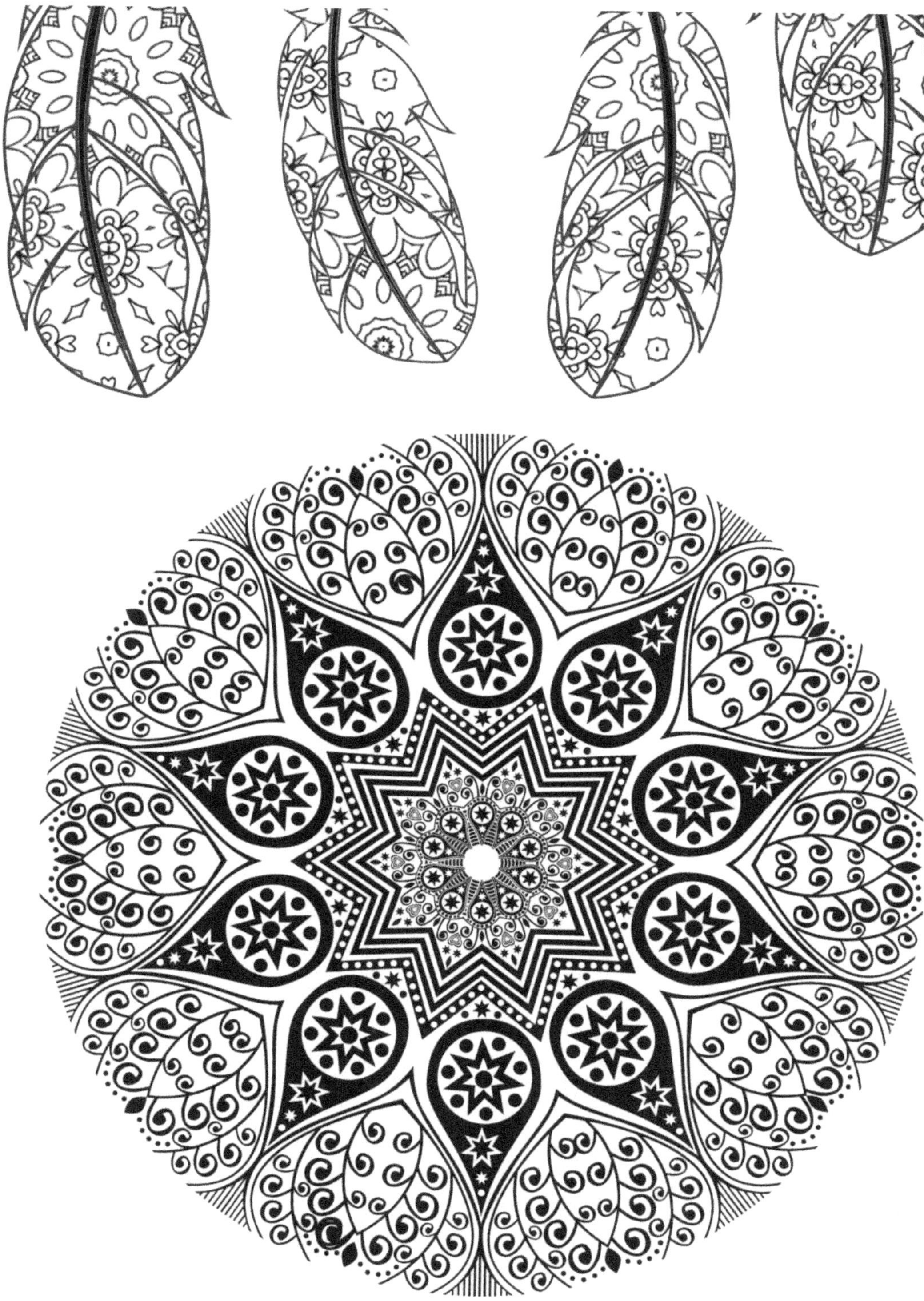

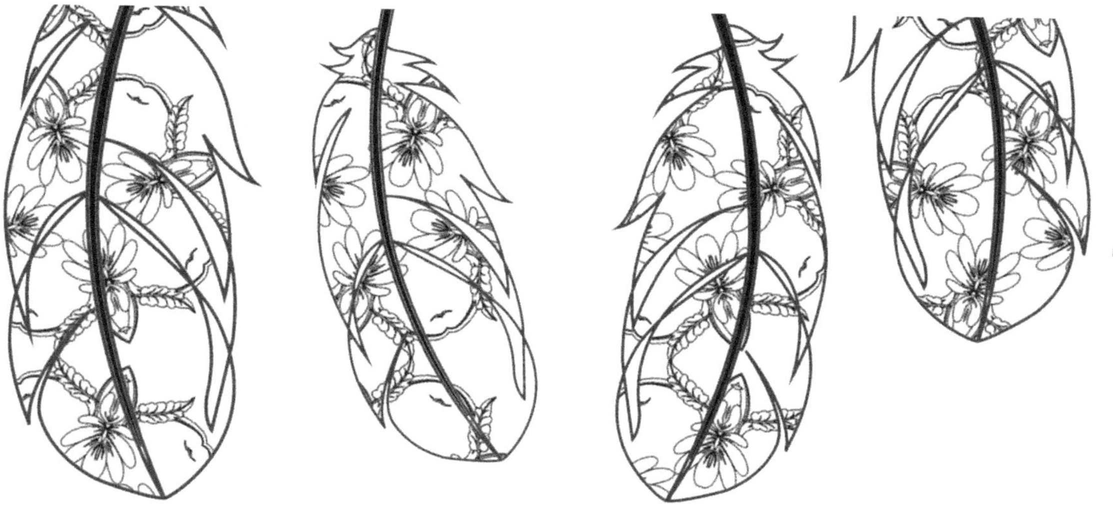

www.ingramcontent.com/pod-product-compliance
Lightning Source LLC
Chambersburg PA
CBHW080552190526
45169CB00007B/2739
9781539489306